EVERYDAY STEM

HOW STREAMING WORKS

PEG ROBINSON

Cavendish Square

New York

Published in 2019 by Cavendish Square Publishing, LLC
243 5th Avenue, Suite 136, New York, NY 10016

Library of Congress Cataloging-in-Publication Data

Names: Robinson, Peg, author.
Title: How streaming works / Peg Robinson.
Description: New York : Cavendish Square, 2019. | Series: Everyday STEM |
Includes bibliographical references and index. |
Identifiers: LCCN 2017051180 (print) | LCCN 2017058806 (ebook) |
ISBN 9781502637598 (ebook) | ISBN 9781502637567 (library bound) |
ISBN 9781502637574 (pbk.) | ISBN 9781502637581 (6 pack)
Subjects: LCSH: Streaming technology (Telecommunications)--Juvenile literature.
Classification: LCC TK5105.386 (ebook) | LCC TK5105.386 .R63 2019 (print) | DDC 006.7--dc23
LC record available at https://lccn.loc.gov/2017051180

Editorial Director: David McNamara
Editor: Meghan Lamb
Copy Editor: Nathan Heidelberger
Associate Art Director: Amy Greenan
Designer: Alan Sliwinski/Christina Shults
Production Coordinator: Karol Szymczuk
Photo Research: J8 Media

Printed in the United States of America

CONTENTS

1 **Streaming Media**................................5

    Good and Bad 10

2 **Making Streaming Work**........................ 17

    Solving a Problem.................... 22

Technology Timeline........................ 28

Glossary 29

Find Out More............................ 30

Index 31

About the Author........................ 32

These happy children are using streaming to watch a movie.

CHAPTER 1
STREAMING MEDIA

What do people mean when they talk about "streaming," or "streaming media"?

You have probably used streaming media every day, even if you did not know what to call it. When you watch a movie on Netflix on your computer, you are watching streaming media. When your parents show you a TV show on a tablet, that is also streaming media. YouTube videos are streaming media. When you and your friends play a game online, you are using streaming media.

Streaming is a special way of **downloading** information. When you download a file, you move it from somewhere else, like the internet, onto your own computer.

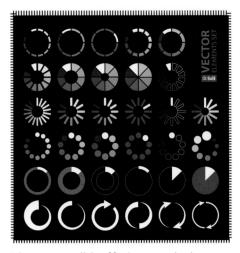

These are all buffering symbols.

Ordinary downloads are kept in permanent **memory**. They can take up a lot of room in your computer.

When you stream a file, you use it right away, while it's downloading. Then, the computer can forget it instead of keeping it. This allows people to watch movies, listen to music, or play games online. Your computer doesn't have to hold entire movies or games.

STREAMING AND STORAGE

For a long time, no one knew how to make streaming work for things like movies.

FAST FACT

On June 24, 1993, the band Severe Tire Damage was the first to perform live online, as part of a promotion of new technological advances that led to the streaming industry.

Streaming allows you to play games and listen to music online.

They treated a movie like one big chunk of information. It took a lot of computer space to make room for a movie

The process of streaming often slowed down, causing the movie to **lag** or stop entirely. This made streaming media very annoying. Then, someone got a clever idea. Instead of sending a whole movie, they chopped the movie up. They sent the movie in small pieces.

Servers allow us to stream online media and save storage space on our computers. This provides us with more options.

When we stream media, we put it into a temporary **buffer**. A buffer is an area on the computer used to store information for a short time. When we use streaming media, a buffer is used to hold our videos, music, and games so we can use them.

Your computer can load just a little piece of information at a time. When your computer uses

GOOD AND BAD

There are good things about streaming media. Streaming allows people to enjoy music and movies and to play games whenever they want them. They do not have to store them in the permanent memory on their computers. They don't

Thanks to streaming, you no longer have to buy hundreds of CDs and DVDs to have access to the movies and music that you love.

have to have hundreds of CDs and DVDs. Streaming makes rental easy, with no need to return your rented media.

One bad part about streaming media is that you can only use it if the internet is working. If the power turns off in your town, the movie you are watching will also turn off. If the internet stops working, your music will also stop.

If you rent a movie or game to stream, you don't own it. You can buy streaming media outright–some services like Amazon give you permanent access to their streaming if you pay a higher price. But you don't keep your own copy.

Musicians, actors, and writers are often paid less for streaming media than media sold in stores. They can be paid much less by streaming services like Spotify.

Dividing files into small bits lets us stream them more easily.

up a piece of information, it sends a message that says "I want the next bit." When the first bit is done, the computer "forgets" that bit. The computer takes the new bit coming in. These small pieces flow together as one. You'd never know the movie was broken up into little bits.

Buffers are like buckets. You can have a big bucket or a little bucket. A small buffer holds less data—or information—than a large buffer. Small buckets are easier to handle than large ones. But many projects are very big.

We have learned to use small buffers the same way you would use a small bucket to empty a big bathtub. We empty a big bathtub one bucket at a time. We use a little bit of media at a time. We can start playing our media

Almost anything we love can be stored in digital form.

before the entire thing downloads.

The Cloud

We have different ways of storing media. One method is to keep things

Small groups of data—or packets—are easiest for our computers to manage.

FAST FACT

Each piece of streaming media sent between a **server** and a computer is called a **packet**. The size of packets is set by real time streaming protocol (RTSP) rules. These rules are like driving rules, or the rules of a game. They make sure everyone works together and everything stays in order.

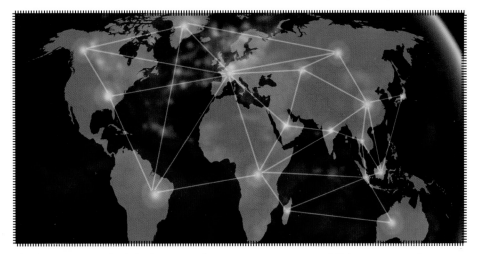

The internet and global servers let you stream material from around the world.

in the **cloud**. The cloud is like an online warehouse. You can store videos, music, and games without using space on your computer. You can send these materials to your computer when you want to use them.

Streaming gives us choices around the world!

CHAPTER 2
MAKING STREAMING WORK

Have you ever seen a relay race? In a relay race, a team of runners takes turns racing. Each runner only finishes part of the race. When the first runner finishes the first part of the race, he or she passes a stick called a baton to another runner. This tells the second runner it is his or her turn to run. After the second runner finishes, he or she passes the baton to the third

A relay racer passes his baton to the next racer. When streaming, a server passes a packet to another computer in the same way.

runner, who passes the baton to the fourth runner, and so on.

Streaming is a little bit like that. In streaming, a server passes a packet to another computer, like a runner passing a baton. But a streaming server has to work with more than one computer. Streaming has to work with many people at once.

Imagine hundreds of runners with hundreds of batons running hundreds of different races. Imagine the many problems that must be solved to make these races work. If the batons are too heavy, the runners will drop them. If no one knows where the race begins and ends, they will not know where to pass the batons.

Computers need rules to maintain the streaming system.

In the same way, many problems needed to be solved to make streaming work.

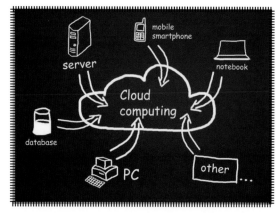

Cloud servers and streaming allow many different devices to share information through the internet.

The first problem is where to keep a movie, a game, or some music so it can be found. When you own a movie, you keep it in your own computer, on a DVD, or in an external drive. But when you stream the movie, someone else keeps it for you. Your computer has to go find it.

This is done using long web addresses called URLs. These work for computers the way your house address or phone number works. An address tells people how to find you and contact you. Web addresses tell computers how to find files.

FINDING AND SENDING INFORMATION

If you rent a movie from a service like Amazon, you go to the main site and choose the movie you want to watch. Then, you click on it. This click connects you to a server. The server may hold hundreds

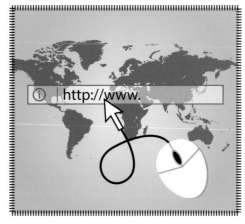

Web addresses, or URLs, help computers find files on the internet.

SOLVING A PROBLEM

Complicated things often work better if they use simple rules to keep things in order. Traffic works better with traffic lights. Cars go on green and stop on red. Everyone watches the lights to make sure we are all safe. Games work better with rules.

Streaming media has rules too. The main rules that make streaming possible are called the real time streaming protocol (RTSP). These were developed by three groups working together.

RTSP rules let us keep track of widespread data.

SOLVING A PROBLEM

Columbia University worked with Netscape and with RealNetworks. They worked out a set of rules for streaming.

Music is one of the most popular forms of streaming media.

These rules allow servers and computers to swap all kinds of information. The rules make sure they have the same information. The servers use different kinds of passwords and commands. This keeps the data safe. Without rules like RTSP, it would be impossible to count on streaming media.

Our current techniques and RTSP protocols allow us to stream faster than ever. You rarely have to wait a long time for a file to load.

of movies. The server has its own addresses that show where the movie is. Your link from Amazon ties you to the exact movie you chose.

Servers

As the internet has grown, so has the use of servers. A server is a special kind of computer that can store lots of information. It can send that information to other computers around the world through the internet. As long as you have an internet connection, servers are available whenever you want.

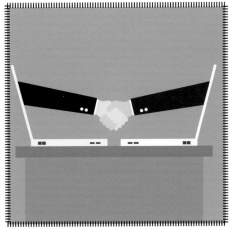

Computer "handshakes" occur as different computers come into contact.

FAST FACT

You don't have to wait for a library or a store to open. Sites like YouTube, Pandora, and Amazon use servers to store lots of videos and songs. You can access them at any time.

Streaming works better because everyone knows the rules.

The size of a packet of data is one of the things set by the RTSP rules. If the size of the packets were not all the same, the computers would have more work to do and the downloads would be slower, with more lags.

RTSP Rules

Engineers and programmers worked out rules called the real time streaming protocol (RTSP). These are rules for sending chunks of information from servers over the internet to your computer. Your computer and the server talk back and forth. They use the RTSP to arrange every data swap. The arrangements are sometimes called **handshakes**.

These rules are like the rules of a game. The rules tell computers when servers start to exchange information. They tell servers how much information to send.

1969 The internet, then known as ARPANET, is established.

1980 Usenet opens the internet to the public.

1992 Starworks, the first commercial streaming service, is launched.

1993 Severe Tire Damage gives first live online concert.

1996 The first worldwide agreement on the rules of streaming is reached: RTSP 1.0.

2007 Netflix introduces its streaming service, expanding its business from sending DVDs through the mail.

buffer Memory holding material to be played.

cloud Servers far away from your own computer where you can store files and access them through the internet.

download The process of sending files over the internet from one computer to another.

handshake When two computers communicate with each other to exchange information.

lag A slow-down or full stop when streaming a movie, game, or song.

memory Hardware that stores information on computers.

packet A portion of information sent from a server to a computer.

server A computer linked to the internet that holds large amounts of information and sends it to other computers.

FIND OUT MORE

BOOKS

Einspruch, Andrew. *Wired World*. New York: PowerKids
    Press, 2013.

Porterfield, Jason. *File Sharing: Rights and Risks*. New York:
    Rosen Digital, 2015.

WEBSITES

How Streaming Video and Audio Work

https://computer.howstuffworks.com/internet/
basics/streaming-video-and-audio.htm

Streaming Media

http://www.explainthatstuff.com/streamingmedia.html

INDEX

Page numbers in **boldface** are illustrations.

buffer, **6**, 9, 13, 25

cloud, 14–15

download, 6–7, 14, 25–26

games, 6–7, 9–11, 15, 20

handshake, **25**, 27

internet, 6–7, 11, 15,
    24–25, 27

lag, 8, 25–26

memory, 6, 10

movies, 5, 7–12, 20–21, 24

music, 7, 9–11, 15, 20, 26

packet, 14, 18, 26

real time streaming protocol
    (RTSP), 14, 22–23, 26–27

relay, 17–19, **18**

rental, 11, 21, 24

rules, 14, 22–23, 26–27

server, **9**, 14, 18–19, 21,
    23–27

URLs, 20–21

Peg Robinson is a writer and editor specializing in researched educational materials and white papers. She graduated with honors from the University of California at Santa Barbara and attended Pacifica Graduate Institution. She served for two years as a docent for Opus Archives, focusing on converting historically significant audio recordings to digital format, securing valuable material in a less fragile recording medium. She lives in Rhode Island with her daughter and her cat and dog.